V I O L I N
ONE HUNDRED
C L A S S I C A L
T H E M E S

Exclusive Distributors:
Music Sales Limited
8/9 Frith Street, London W1V 5TZ, England.
Music Sales Corporation
257 Park Avenue South, New York, NY10010, USA.
Music Sales Pty Limited
120 Rothschild Avenue, Rosebery, NSW 2018, Australia.

This book © Copyright 1991 by Wise Publications
Order No. AM84153
ISBN 0-7119-2587-9

Design by Hutton Staniford
Front cover photography by Stuart MacGregor

Music Sales' complete catalogue lists thousands of titles
and is free from your local music shop, or direct from
Music Sales Limited.
Please send a cheque/postal order for £1.50 for postage to:
Music Sales Limited, Newmarket Road, Bury St. Edmunds,
Suffolk IP33 3YB.

Your Guarantee of Quality
As publishers, we strive to produce every book to the
highest commercial standards.
The music has been freshly engraved and the book has
been carefully designed to minimise awkward page turns
and to make playing from it a real pleasure.
Particular care has been given to specifying acid-free,
neutral-sized paper which has not been elemental chlorine bleached
but produced with special regard for the environment.
Throughout, the printing and binding have been planned
to ensure a sturdy, attractive publication which should
give years of enjoyment.
If your copy fails to meet our high standards, please inform
us and we will gladly replace it.

Printed in the United Kingdom by
Caligraving Limited, Thetford, Norfolk.

Wise Publications
London/New York/Sydney

A MUSICAL JOKE

(K.522, 4th movement) Mozart

A POLICEMAN'S LOT IS NOT A HAPPY ONE

('The Pirates of Penzance') Sullivan

AIR ON THE G STRING

(Suite No.3, 2nd movement) Bach

AUTUMN

(The Four Seasons, No.3, 1st movement) Vivaldi

AUTUMN

(The Four Seasons, No.3, 3rd movement) Vivaldi

BARCAROLLE

('The Tales Of Hoffmann') Offenbach

BERCEUSE

(Dolly Suite Op.56) Fauré

Allegretto moderato

BOLERO

Ravel

Tempo di Bolero moderato assai ♩=72

BRIDAL MARCH

('Lohengrin') Wagner

Moderato con moto

BRIGG FAIR

(An English Rhapsody) Delius

With easy movement ♩.=66
Allegretto leggiero

BRINDISI

('La Traviata') Verdi

CHE FARÒ SENZA EURIDICE

('Orfeo ed Euridice') Gluck

Andante con moto

CLARINET CONCERTO

(K.622, 2nd movement) Mozart

Adagio

CLAIRE DE LUNE

(Suite Bergamasque) Debussy

EINE KLEINE NACHTMUSIK

(K.525, 1st movement) Mozart

EMPEROR WALTZ

(op.437) Strauss

Tempo di valse

ben legato

ESPAÑA

(Rhapsody for Orchestra) Chabrier

Allegro con fuoco (♩.=80)

FARANDOLE

(L'Arlésienne Suite No.2) Bizet

Allegro vivo e deciso

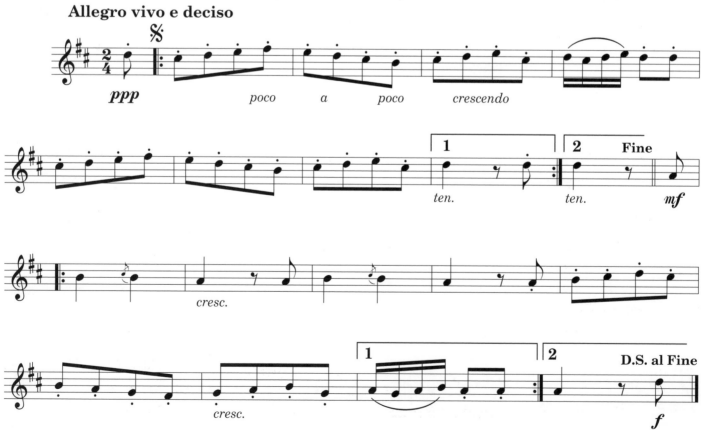

FOR HE IS AN ENGLISHMAN

('HMS Pinafore') Sullivan

FÜR ELISE

Beethoven

GALOP INFERNAL

('Orpheus in the Underworld') Offenbach

GAUDEAMUS IGITUR

(Academic Festival Overture Op.80) Brahms

GAVOTTE

(Suite No.3, 3rd movement) Bach

GOLLIWOGG'S CAKE WALK

(Children's Corner) Debussy

Allegro giusto

GYMNOPÉDIE NO.1

Satie

Lent et douloureux

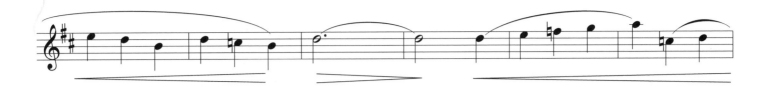

HABAÑERA

('Carmen') Bizet

Allegretto quasi andantino

HE SHALL FEED HIS FLOCK

('The Messiah') Handel

Larghetto e piano

HORN CONCERTO NO.4

(K.495, 3rd movement) Mozart

Allegro vivace

HORNPIPE

(The Water Music) Handel

Alla Hornpipe

HUMORESQUE

(Op.101 No.7) Dvořák

Poco lento e grazioso

HUNGARIAN DANCE NO.5

Brahms

JERUSALEM

Parry

JUPITER – I VOW TO THEE, MY COUNTRY

(The Planets Suite) Holst

LA CALINDA

('Koanga') Delius

Moderato, con grazia

LÀ CI DAREM LA MANO

('Don Giovanni') Mozart

Andante

24

LA DONNA È MOBILE

('Rigoletto') Verdi

LAND OF HOPE AND GLORY

(Pomp & Circumstance March No.1 Op.39) Elgar

Allegro (largamente)

LARGO - OMBRA MAI FÙ

('Xerxes') Handel

LES SYLPHIDES

(Prelude Op.28 No.7) Chopin

MARCH

(The Nutcracker Suite Op.71) Tchaikovsky

MINUET II

(Music for the Royal Fireworks) Handel

MORNING

(Peer Gynt Suite No.1 Op.46) Grieg

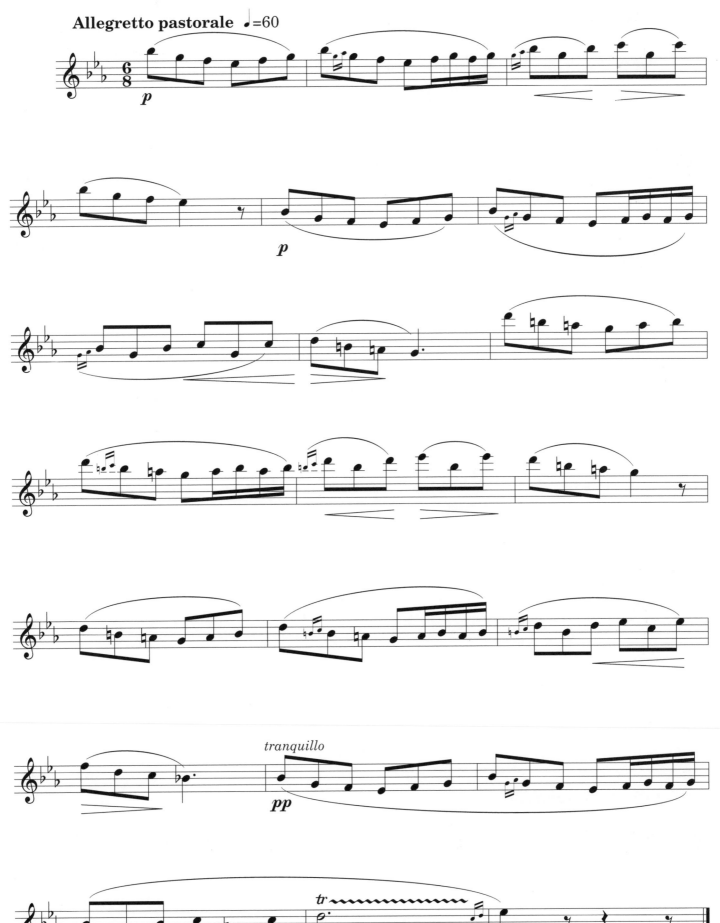

NIMROD

(Enigma Variations Op.36) Elgar

NOCTURNE

('A Midsummer Night's Dream' Op.61) Mendelssohn

NON PIÙ ANDRAI

('The Marriage of Figaro') Mozart

O FOR THE WINGS OF A DOVE

('Hear My Prayer') Mendelssohn

Con moto

ODE TO JOY

(Symphony No.9 Op.125, 4th movement) Beethoven

ONE FINE DAY

('Madame Butterfly') Puccini

PAVANE

(Op.50) Fauré

Allegro moderato

PIANO CONCERTO

(Op.16, 1st movement) Grieg

Allegro molto moderato ♩=84

PIANO CONCERTO – 'ELVIRA MADIGAN'

(K.467, 2nd movement) Mozart

PIANO CONCERTO NO.1

(Op.23, 1st movement) Tchaikovsky

Allegro non troppo e molto maestoso

PIANO CONCERTO NO.3

(Op.37, 1st movement) Beethoven

Allegro con brio

PIANO CONCERTO NO.5 – 'THE EMPEROR'

(Op.73, 2nd movement) Beethoven

Adagio un poco mosso

POLOVTSIAN DANCES

('Prince Igor') Borodin

PIE JESU

(Requiem Op.48) Fauré

POMP & CIRCUMSTANCE MARCH NO.4

(Op.39) Elgar

POOR WAND'RING ONE

('The Pirates Of Penzance') Sullivan

PRELUDE

(L'Arlésienne Suite No.1) Bizet

Allegro deciso (tempo di marcia)

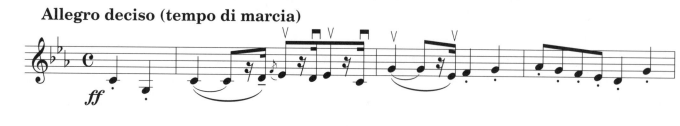

PRELUDE TO ACT III

('Lohengrin') Wagner

Molto vivace

PROMENADE

(Pictures At An Exhibition) Mussorgsky

Allegro giusto, nel modo russico; senza allegrezza, ma poco sostenuto

PRINCE IGOR OVERTURE

Borodin

Allegro

RADETSKY MARCH

(Op.228) Strauss

Allegro moderato

42

ROMEO AND JULIET

(Fantasy Overture) Tchaikovsky

Allegro giusto

RONDEAU

('Abdelazar') Purcell

ROSAMUNDE

(Entr'acte Act III) Schubert

44

SALUT D'AMOUR

(Op.12) Elgar

Andantino

SERENADE

Schubert

Moderato

SPARTACUS – 'THE ONEDIN LINE'

Khatchaturian

SPRING

(The Four Seasons, No.1, 1st movement) Vivaldi

ST ANTHONY CHORALE

(Variations on a Theme of Haydn Op.56a) Brahms

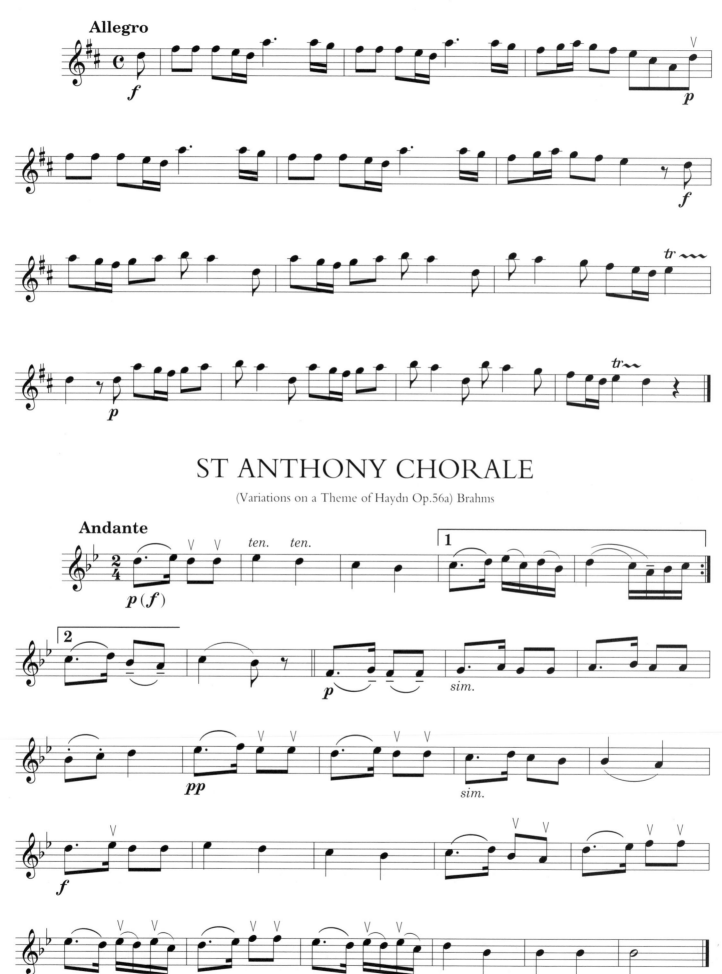

SWAN LAKE

(Op.20, Opening of Act II) Tchaikovsky

SYMPHONIE FANTASTIQUE

(Op.14, 4th movement) Berlioz

SYMPHONY NO.1

(Op.68, 4th movement) Brahms

Allegro non troppo ma con brio

SYMPHONY NO.3

(Op.90, 3rd movement) Brahms

Poco allegretto

SYMPHONY NO.3 – 'THE EROICA'

(Op.55, 2nd movement)

SYMPHONY NO.5

(Op.64, 2nd movement) Tchaikovsky

SYMPHONY NO.6 – 'THE PASTORAL'

(Op.68, 5th movement) Beethoven

SYMPHONY NO.6 – 'THE PATHÉTIQUE'

(Op.74, 1st movement) Tchaikovsky

(teneramente, molto cantabile, con espressione)

SYMPHONY NO.9 – 'THE GREAT'

(2nd movement) Schubert

SYMPHONY NO.9 – 'NEW WORLD'

(Op.95, 2nd movement) Dvořák

SYMPHONY NO.9 – 'NEW WORLD'

(Op.95, 4th movement) Dvořák

SYMPHONY No.94 – 'THE SURPRISE'

(2nd movement) Haydn

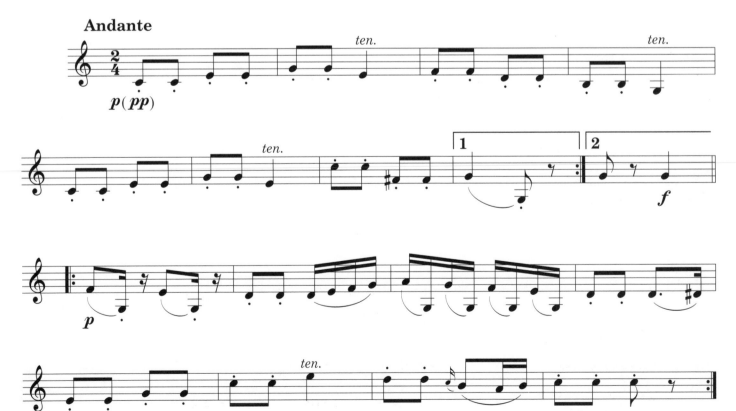

TAKE A PAIR OF SPARKLING EYES

('The Gondoliers') Sullivan

Allegretto moderato

TANNHÄUSER OVERTURE

Wagner

Andante maestoso

tenuto molto

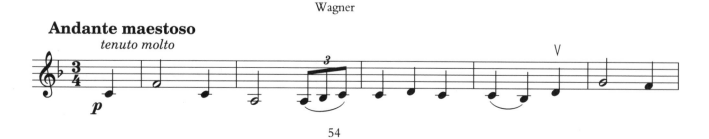

THE BLUE DANUBE

(Waltz, Op.314) Strauss

Tempo di valse

THE MERRY PEASANT

(Album for the Young Op.68 No.10) Schumann

Lively and cheerful

THE TROUT PIANO QUINTET

(4th movement) Schubert

Andantino

TOREADOR'S SONG

('Carmen') Bizet

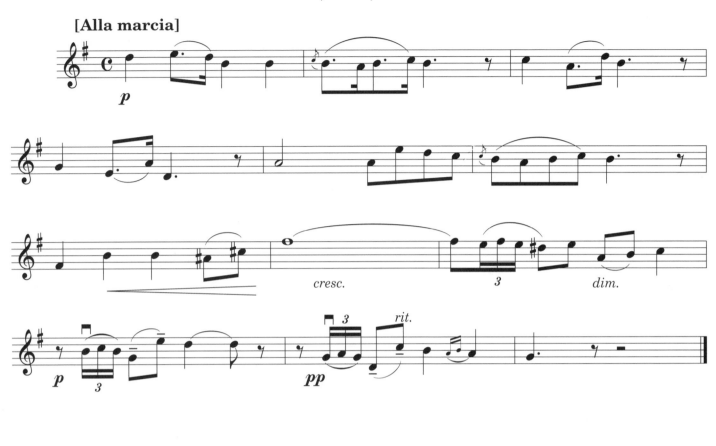

Tristesse

(Étude Op.10 No.3) Chopin

TRUMPET VOLUNTARY

('The Prince of Denmark's March') Clarke

VALSE

('Coppélia') Delibes

VIOLIN CONCERTO

(Op.77, 2nd movement) Brahms

Adagio

VIOLIN CONCERTO

(Op.61, 2nd movement) Elgar

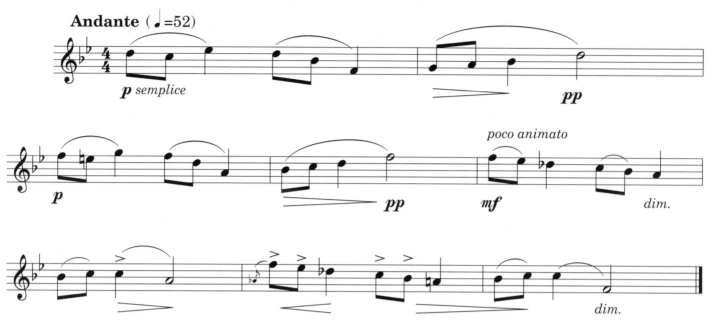

VIOLIN CONCERTO

(Op.64, 2nd movement) Mendelssohn

WALTZ

('The Sleeping Beauty' Op.66) Tchaikovsky

Allegro (tempo di valse)

WEDDING MARCH

('A Midsummer Night's Dream' Op.61) Mendelssohn

WILLIAM TELL OVERTURE

Rossini

YOUR TINY HAND IS FROZEN

('La Bohème') Puccini

24TH CAPRICE FOR SOLO VIOLIN

Paganini

11/99 (35789)